Senior Care

Cognitive Enrichment Worksheets

SENIOR CARE
COGNITIVE ENRICHMENT WORKSHEETS

Written and created by Sally Safadi

Published by Neurons Away LLC
Syracuse, New York
Copyright © 2024 NeuronsAway

All rights reserved worldwide. No part of this publication may be reproduced in any material form (including photocopying of any pages other than the illustrated handouts, storing it in any medium by electronic means and wether or not transiently or incidentally to some other use of this publication) without the written permission of the copyright owner. Application's for the copyright owner's written permission to reproduce any part of this publication should be adressed to the publisher. All illustrated handouts may be photocopied for personal use for this program, but may not reproduced for any other purpose without the permission of the publisher.

Warning: The doing of an unauthorized act in relation to a copyright work may result in both a civil claim for damages and criminal prosecution.

ISBN: 978-1-943825-18-9

NAME_____

Get ready to spark memories, boost your brain, and enjoy every moment—

this workbook is all about *you*!

If you could spend a day with any animal, what animal would you choose, and what would you do together?

What do you want to learn from this animal?
_____
_____

Have you ever had a pet? What was their name, and what did you enjoy doing with them?
_____
_____
_____

Draw a picture of you and your animal.

NAME_____

SENIOR CARE COGNITIVE ENRICHMENT WORKSHEETS

Imagine you're sitting on a beautiful beach. What sounds and smells would you experience?

Close your eyes and describe what the waves might sound like—what the sun might feel like.

_____
_____
_____

Have you ever visited the beach? What was your favorite thing to do there?

_____
_____
_____

Draw the waves or the seashells on the beach.

NAME_____

SENIOR CARE COGNITIVE ENRICHMENT WORKSHEETS

If you could plant a magical garden, what kinds of flowers and plants would grow there?

Describe the colors in your magical garden.

_____
_____
_____

Have you ever grown flowers or vegetables in a garden? What did you grow?

_____
_____
_____
_____
_____
_____
_____

Draw the largest or most colorful flower in your magical garden.

NAME_____   ©NeuronsAway

What would your favorite day look like from morning to night?

Describe what you would do in the afternoon of your perfect day.

_____
_____
_____

Do you remember a day that felt perfect? What made it so special?

_____
_____
_____

Draw what you see outside during your perfect day.

If you could fly like a bird, where would you go and what would you see from above?

Draw what you might see in the sky.

Have you ever flown in an airplane? Where did you go?

_____

_____

Draw the sky, clouds, or mountains you'd fly over.

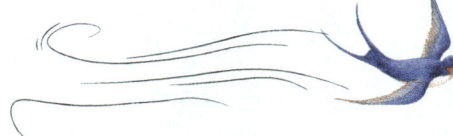

SENIOR CARE COGNITIVE ENRICHMENT WORKSHEETS

What's the best dream you've ever had? How did it make you feel?

How would you describe the colors or shapes in your dream?

_____
_____
_____
_____
_____

What was the last dream you can remember having?

_____
_____
_____
_____
_____

Draw a picture from your dream.

NAME_____

SENIOR CARE COGNITIVE ENRICHMENT WORKSHEETS

If you could eat one meal every day for the rest of your life, what would it be, and why?

Describe the flavors of your favorite meal.

_____
_____
_____

Who made your favorite meal for you when you were younger?

_____
_____
_____

Draw the meal you would love to eat every day.

SENIOR CARE COGNITIVE ENRICHMENT WORKSHEETS

If you could travel back to your favorite childhood memory, where would you go?

What was the weather like in your favorite memory?

_____
_____

Who were you with in that memory? What did you enjoy doing together?

_____
_____
_____

Draw the place where this memory happened.

SENIOR CARE COGNITIVE ENRICHMENT WORKSHEETS

Imagine you find a magical door in your home. Where does it lead, and what do you discover?

What would you bring with you on this adventure?
_____
_____
_____

Draw the magical door.

Draw what you see when you open the door.

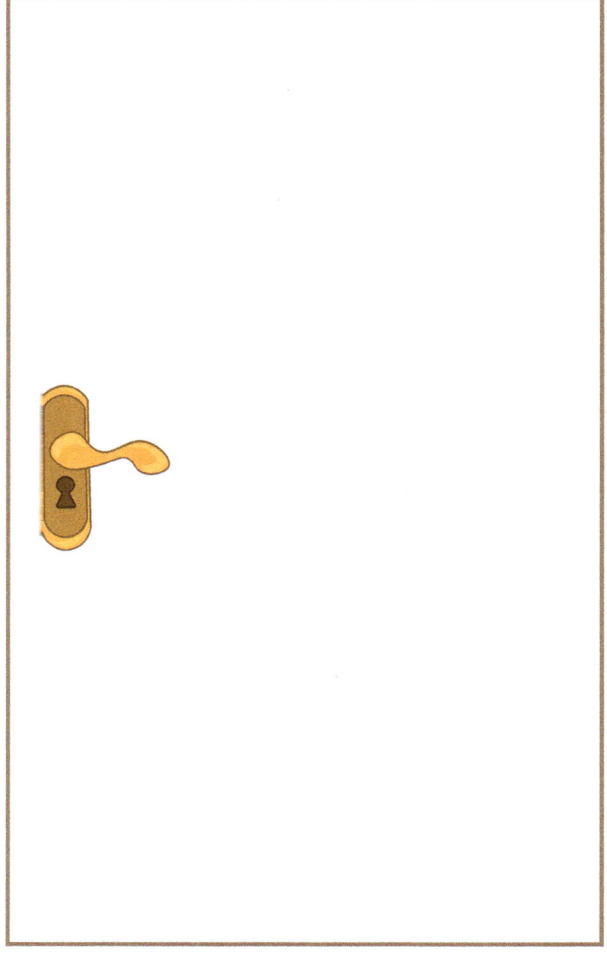

NAME_____

What color makes you feel the happiest? Why does it make you feel that way?

What other things are that color (flowers, objects, clothes)?

_____
_____
_____

Draw something in your favorite color.

Draw something in your favorite color that makes you feel happy.

SENIOR CARE COGNITIVE ENRICHMENT WORKSHEETS

What is your favorite childhood song or nursery rhyme? Can you say or sing part of it?

Describe where you learned the rhyme or song.

_____
_____
_____
_____

Can you clap or tap along to the rhythm?

🖍 Draw a picture of something that reminds you of the rhyme or song.

SENIOR CARE COGNITIVE ENRICHMENT WORKSHEETS

 **If you could cook a meal with your family, what would you make together?**

What ingredients would you need for this meal?
_____
_____

Did you ever help someone cook when you were younger? What did you make?
_____
_____
_____

Draw the meal you would make with your family.

NAME_____

SENIOR CARE COGNITIVE ENRICHMENT WORKSHEETS

Describe your favorite holiday tradition. How did you and your family celebrate?

What was the best part of the holiday? Was there a specific food or event you loved?

_____
_____
_____

Did you ever travel for holidays? Where did you go?

_____
_____

Draw something that reminds you of your favorite holiday.

SENIOR CARE COGNITIVE ENRICHMENT WORKSHEETS

What would you grow in a vegetable garden? Have you ever grown your own food?

What vegetables or fruits would you pick first from your garden?

_____
_____
_____

Did your family have a garden when you were a child? What did you grow?

_____
_____
_____

Draw a picture of your vegetable garden.

NAME_____

SENIOR CARE COGNITIVE ENRICHMENT WORKSHEETS

What did you love doing outdoors when you were young? Did you have a favorite place to go?

Describe what the air fe t like in your favorite outdoor place?

_____
_____
_____
_____
_____

Did you go camping or hiking? What did you enjoy most about being in nature?

_____
_____
_____
_____
_____

Draw the outdoor place you loved visiting.

SENIOR CARE COGNITIVE ENRICHMENT WORKSHEETS

Can you name your favorite piece of clothing? How did it make you feel when you wore it?

What color was your favorite piece of clothing?
_____

Did you wear it for a special occasion or every day?
_____

  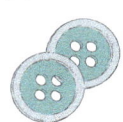

Draw the piece of clothing you loved to wear.

What was your first job? How did it feel to earn your first paycheck?

What kind of work did you do, and did you enjoy it?
_____
_____
_____

What did you buy with your first paycheck?
_____
_____
_____

Draw something related to your first job.

NAME_____

SENIOR CARE COGNITIVE ENRICHMENT WORKSHEETS

What's the most memorable gift you've ever received? Who gave it to you?

How did you feel when you received the gift?

_____
_____
_____

Did you ever give someone a special gift in return?

_____
_____
_____

Draw the gift you received.

NAME_____

SENIOR CARE COGNITIVE ENRICHMENT WORKSHEETS

Can you describe the home you grew up in? What was your favorite room?

What color were the walls or floor in your favorite room?
_____

Who did you spend the most time with in that room?
_____
_____
_____

Draw your favorite room.

SENIOR CARE COGNITIVE ENRICHMENT WORKSHEETS

What was the first movie you remember seeing? How did it make you feel?

Did you go to a theater, or did you watch it at home?

_____

Did you see the movie with anyone special? What was that person's reaction?

_____
_____

Draw a scene from the movie you saw.

If you could share a meal with someone famous, who would it be and what would you talk about?

What meal would you want to share with them?
_____

Would you ask them for advice or tell them about your life?
_____
_____
_____

Draw the meal you would share with this person.

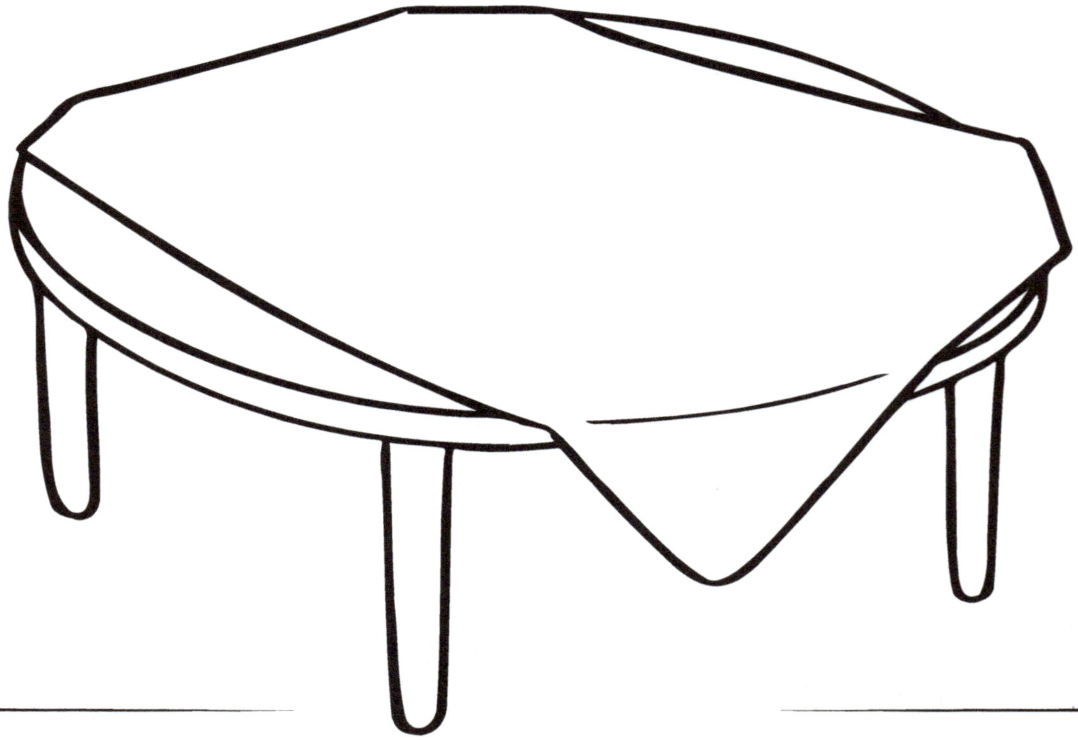

SENIOR CARE COGNITIVE ENRICHMENT WORKSHEETS

 **What is one smell that brings back happy memories? Where were you when you first smelled it?**

What time of year was it when you smelled this scent?

_____

What other things that remind you of this memory?

_____
_____

Draw the thing that created the smell.

NAME_____ ©NeuronsAway

SENIOR CARE COGNITIVE ENRICHMENT WORKSHEETS

Do you have a favorite season of the year? What do you love about it?

What do you like to wear during your favorite season?

_____
_____
_____

What activities did you enjoy during that season?

_____
_____
_____

Draw something from your favorite season.

SENIOR CARE COGNITIVE ENRICHMENT WORKSHEETS

What kind of music makes you want to dance? Can you describe a time when you danced and felt free?

Where were you, and who did you dance with?

_____
_____
_____

Hum or tap along to a song that makes you want to dance.

Draw what you look like when you're dancing.

SENIOR CARE COGNITIVE ENRICHMENT WORKSHEETS

What was your favorite family recipe growing up? Did you ever help make it?

Who taught you how to make it, or who made it best?

_____

What ingredients were needed to make this recipe?

_____
_____
_____
_____
_____
_____
_____

Draw the recipe or the meal itself.

SENIOR CARE COGNITIVE ENRICHMENT WORKSHEETS

Describe the first time you saw snow (or your favorite weather event)?

How did the snow (or weather) make you feel when you saw it?

_____

Did you ever play in the snow or rain? What games did you play?

_____
_____
_____
_____
_____
_____
_____

Draw the snow or weather event.

NAME_____

SENIOR CARE COGNITIVE ENRICHMENT WORKSHEETS

What game did you enjoy playing with friends or siblings as a child? How did you feel when you played it?

Describe how the game was played
_____
_____
_____

Who was your favorite person to play with?
_____

Draw something related to the game.

If you could design your dream vacation, where would you go, and what would you do there?

What would you pack for your dream vacation?

_____
_____
_____
_____
_____

What kind of food would you eat on your trip?

_____
_____
_____
_____
_____

Draw a place you would visit on this vacation.

If you had a magical power for one day, what would it be, and how would you use it?

Would you use your power to help others? How?
_____
_____
_____

Would you want to fly, be invisible, or something else? Why?
_____
_____

Draw yourself using your magical power.

SENIOR CARE COGNITIVE ENRICHMENT WORKSHEETS

If you could relive one joyful moment from your past, what would it be, and why?

Who was with you during that joyful moment?
_____
_____

Can you describe what made that moment so special?
_____
_____
_____

Draw the moment you would relive.

SENIOR CARE COGNITIVE ENRICHMENT WORKSHEETS

Can you describe your favorite holiday celebration? What made it special?

What kind of food did your family enjoy during holidays?

_____
_____

Did your family have any unique traditions?

_____
_____
_____

Draw a memory from a favorite holiday celebration.

NAME_____ ©NeuronsAway

If you could visit any place, real or imaginary, where would you go?

Who would you want to visit this place with?
_____

What would you want to see or do in this place?
_____
_____
_____

Draw the place you'd love to visit.

SENIOR CARE COGNITIVE ENRICHMENT WORKSHEETS

If you could build your dream house anywhere in the world, where would it be, and what would it look like?

Describe what rooms would be in your dream house.

_____
_____
_____
_____

What color would you paint the outside of your dream house? _____

Draw your dream house.

SENIOR CARE COGNITIVE ENRICHMENT WORKSHEETS

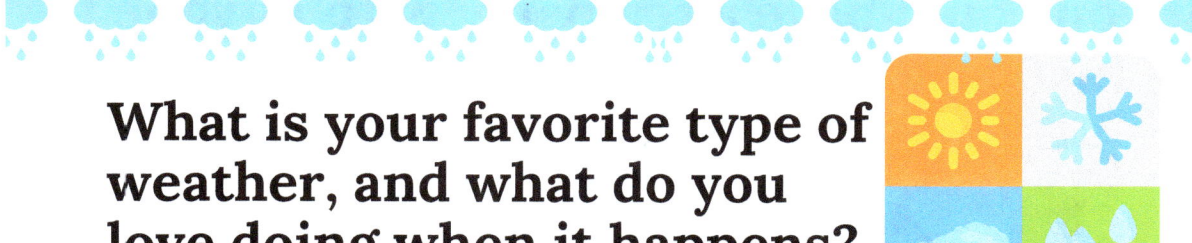

What is your favorite type of weather, and what do you love doing when it happens?

Describe the sound or smell of your favorite weather.

_____
_____

Describe a special day with your favorite kind of weather.

_____
_____
_____

Draw what it looks like outside during your favorite weather.

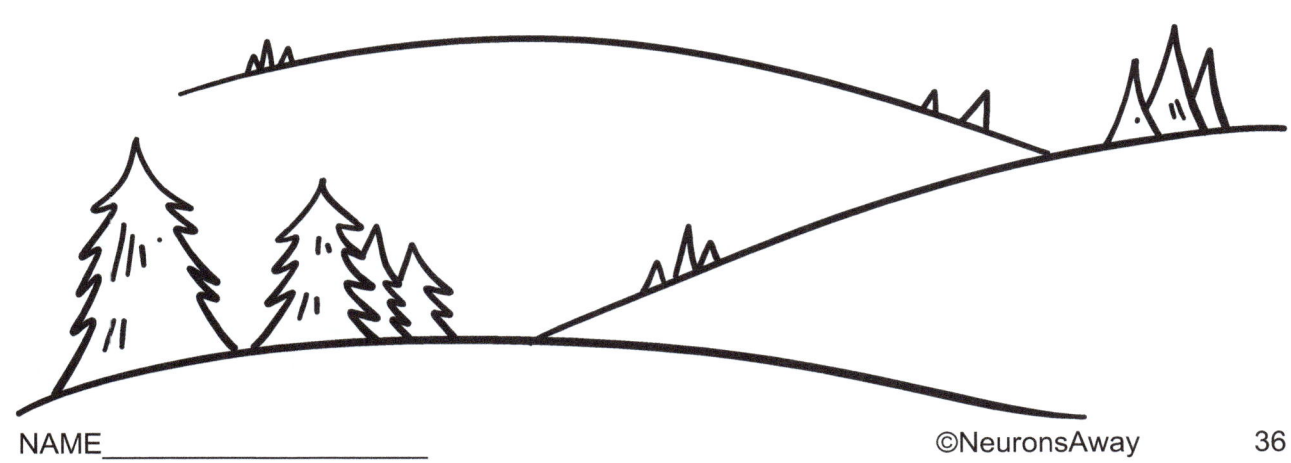

NAME_____

If you could have a tea party with anyone from history or fiction, who would you invite, and what would you serve?

What would you ask your guest during the tea party?

_____
_____

What kind of tea or
dr nk would you serve?

_____
_____

Draw your tea party setup.

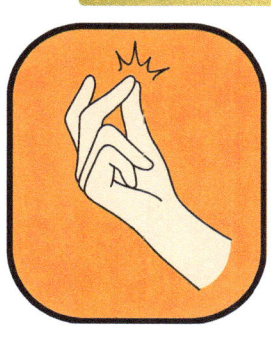

Imagine you could travel anywhere by simply snapping your fingers, where would you go?

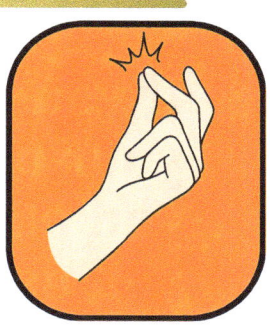

What food would you try in the place you visit?
_____
_____

Who would you bring with you, or who would you meet there?
_____
_____

Draw the place you would visit?

NAME_____

If you could grow any food in your backyard, what would you plant, and how would you use it?

What kind of meals would you make with the food you grow?
_____
_____

Have you ever grown your own food? What did you grow?
_____
_____
_____

Draw the food in your backyard garden.

SENIOR CARE COGNITIVE ENRICHMENT WORKSHEETS

If you could be any character from a book or movie, who would you choose, and why?

What would you do if you were this character for a day?

_____
_____
_____

What is your favorite scene or part of the book/movie this character is from?

_____
_____

 Draw yourself as this character.

NAME_____

SENIOR CARE COGNITIVE ENRICHMENT WORKSHEETS

 **If the rain could be any color other than clear, what color would you like it to be?**

How would the world look different if the rain was this color?

_____
_____

What would you like to do in this colorful rain?

_____
_____

Draw what the colorful rain would look like.

SENIOR CARE COGNITIVE ENRICHMENT WORKSHEETS

Imagine you could spend a day in a beautiful garden. What would it look like, and what would you do there?

What flowers or plants would you want to see in the garden?

_____
_____
_____

What would you do while relaxing in the garden?

_____
_____
_____

Draw the garden you'd love to visit.

SENIOR CARE COGNITIVE ENRICHMENT WORKSHEETS

If you could make a cake for someone special, what kind of cake would it be and how would you decorate it?

What flavors would you choose for the cake?
_____
_____
_____

Who would you make the cake for? _____
_____
_____

Draw the cake and how it would look when decorated.

Imagine you could turn any object in your home into gold. What would you choose, and why?

What would you do with the golden object?
_____
_____
_____

Why is this object special to you?
_____
_____

Draw the object turned into gold.

NAME_____

If you could relive one holiday or celebration from your life, which one would it be?

Who were you with during this celebration?
_____
_____
_____

What activities or food made the celebration memorable?
_____
_____
_____

Draw a scene from that holiday or celebration.

If you could have a pet from any time in your life, which one would you choose and what made them special?

What kind of animal was your pet, and what was its name?
_____

What did you enjoy doing with your pet?
_____
_____

Draw a picture of your pet.

 **Imagine you have wings. Where would you fly, and what would you look forward to seeing from the sky?**

What would the world look like from up high?
_____
_____
_____

What places would you fly to and visit?
_____
_____
_____

Draw a picture of yourself with wings.

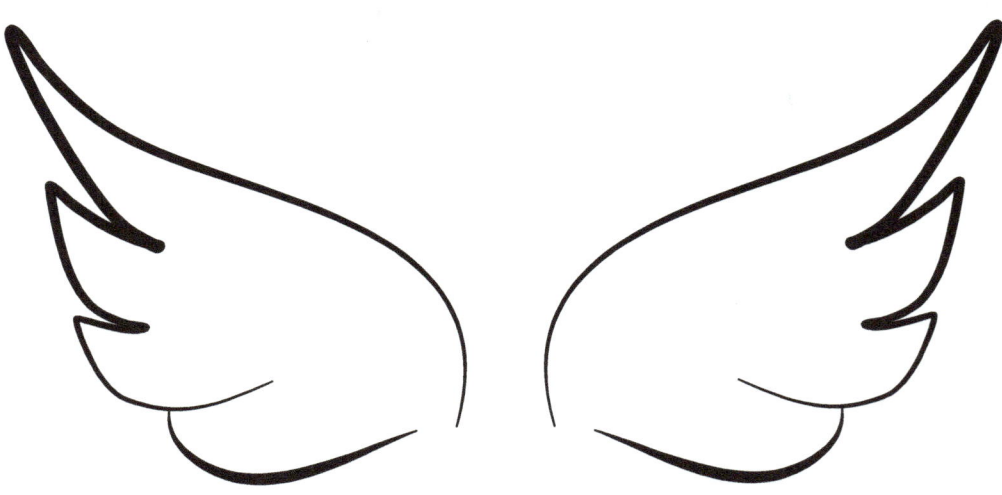

SENIOR CARE COGNITIVE ENRICHMENT WORKSHEETS

What's the most beautiful place you've ever visited? What made it memorable?

What made this place so beautiful for you?

_____
_____
_____

Who were you with when you
visited, or were you alone? _____

Draw what the most beautiful place you have visited.

NAME_____

If you could swim in any body of water (a river, a lake, an ocean), which one would you choose and why?

What does the water feel like as you swim?

_____
_____

Do you have a favorite memory of swimming in one of these places?

_____
_____
_____

Draw yourself swimming in the body of water you chose.

If you could host a magical dinner party, what kind of food would you serve, and who would you invite?

What kind of magical or special food would you serve?

_____

_____

Would you invite family, friends, or someone famous? Why?

_____

_____

Draw your magical dinner party table.

NAME_____

What is your favorite type of flower, and where would you plant this flower?

What color is your favorite flower? _____

Have you ever planted this flower in a garden before?

_____
_____
_____

Draw your favorite flower.

NAME_____

SENIOR CARE COGNITIVE ENRICHMENT WORKSHEETS

If you could bake a magical pie that made people smile, what ingredients would you use?

What special or magical ingredients would make people smile?

_____
_____
_____
_____

Who would you share your magical pie with?

_____
_____
_____
_____

Draw what the magical pie would look like.

SENIOR CARE COGNITIVE ENRICHMENT WORKSHEETS

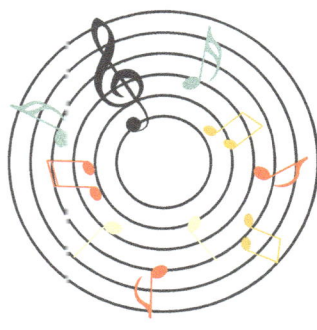
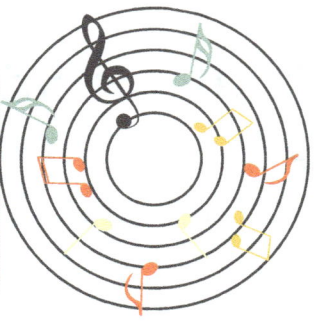

What song brings back the best memories for you, and where were you when you first heard it?

Hum or sing part of the song

What makes this song special to you?

_____
_____
_____
_____
_____
_____

Draw something that reminds you of this song.

SENIOR CARE COGNITIVE ENRICHMENT WORKSHEETS

If you could take a trip on a boat anywhere in the world, where would you want to go, and who would you take with you?

What kind of boat would you want to travel on? ♥
_____
_____

What places would you visit on your trip? ♥
_____
_____

Draw the boat and the place you'd travel to.

If you could wake up tomorrow with a new skill or talent, what would it be?

What would you do with this new skill or talent?
_____
_____

Is there someone who inspired you to want this talent?
_____
_____

Draw yourself using this new skill.

SENIOR CARE COGNITIVE ENRICHMENT WORKSHEETS

Imagine you could paint the sky any color you want. What color would it be, and why?

How would the world look different with this sky color?

_____
_____
_____

Would you choose a different color for each time of day?

_____

Draw the sky in the color you chose.

NAME_____

My Special Recipe

Write down a recipe for a dish that brings back good memories. Include the ingredients, steps, and why it's special to you.

_____
_____
_____
_____
_____
_____
_____
_____
_____

How does it look?

SENIOR CARE COGNITIVE ENRICHMENT WORKSHEETS

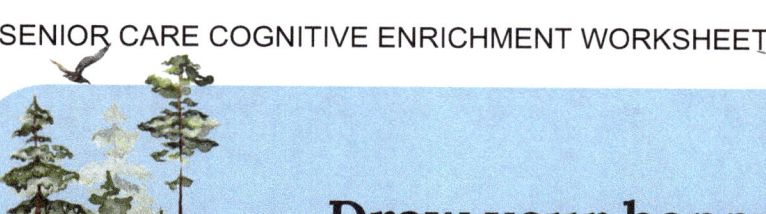

Draw your happy place

Think of a place where you feel peaceful and happy. Draw or describe it, including the sounds, colors, and scents that make it special.

NAME_____   ©NeuronsAway

Imaginative Storytelling

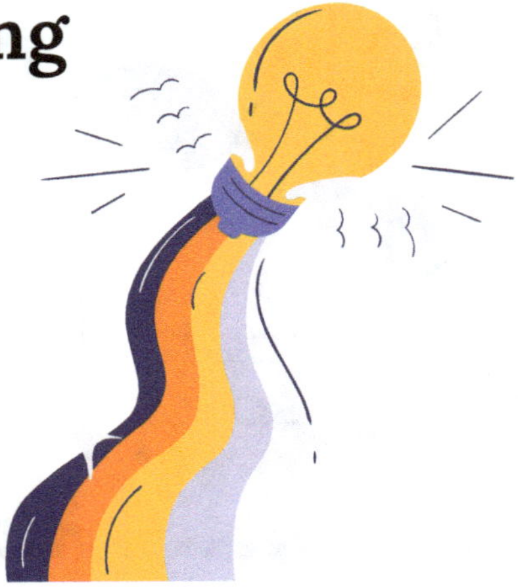

Write the beginning of a story using this sentence: **"One day, I opened the door and found..."** Then, let your imagination take over and complete the story.

NAME_____________________

Your Perfect Day

Imagine your perfect day. What would you do from morning to night? Write or draw how your ideal day would look.

_____
_____
_____
_____
_____
_____

Write a short poem or song using these words: sun, memory, smile, and time. It doesn't have to rhyme—just have fun creating!

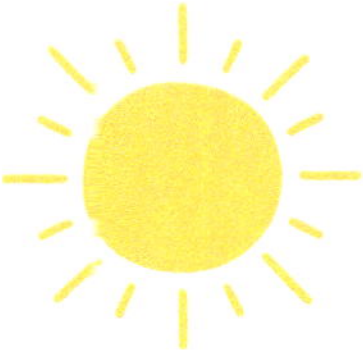

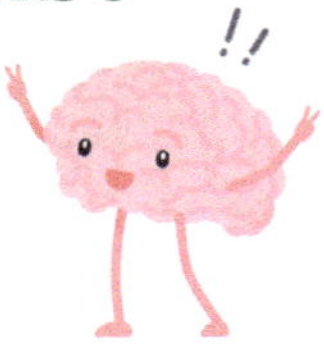

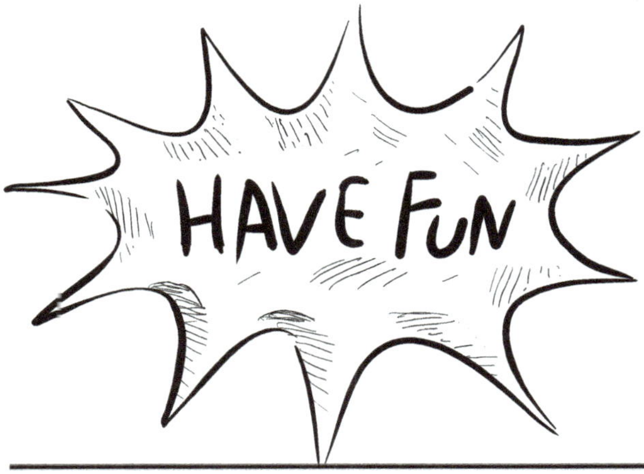

NAME____________________

MEMORY TREE

Draw a tree and write a happy memory on each leaf. These can be moments with friends, family, or special life experiences.

SENIOR CARE COGNITIVE ENRICHMENT WORKSHEETS

Invent a New Object

Imagine you can invent something to make life easier. What would it be? Explain what it does

_____
_____
_____

Draw how it looks.

**Imagine you're making a collage of your favorite life moments.
Write down or sketch four things you would include—places, people, objects, or experiences.**

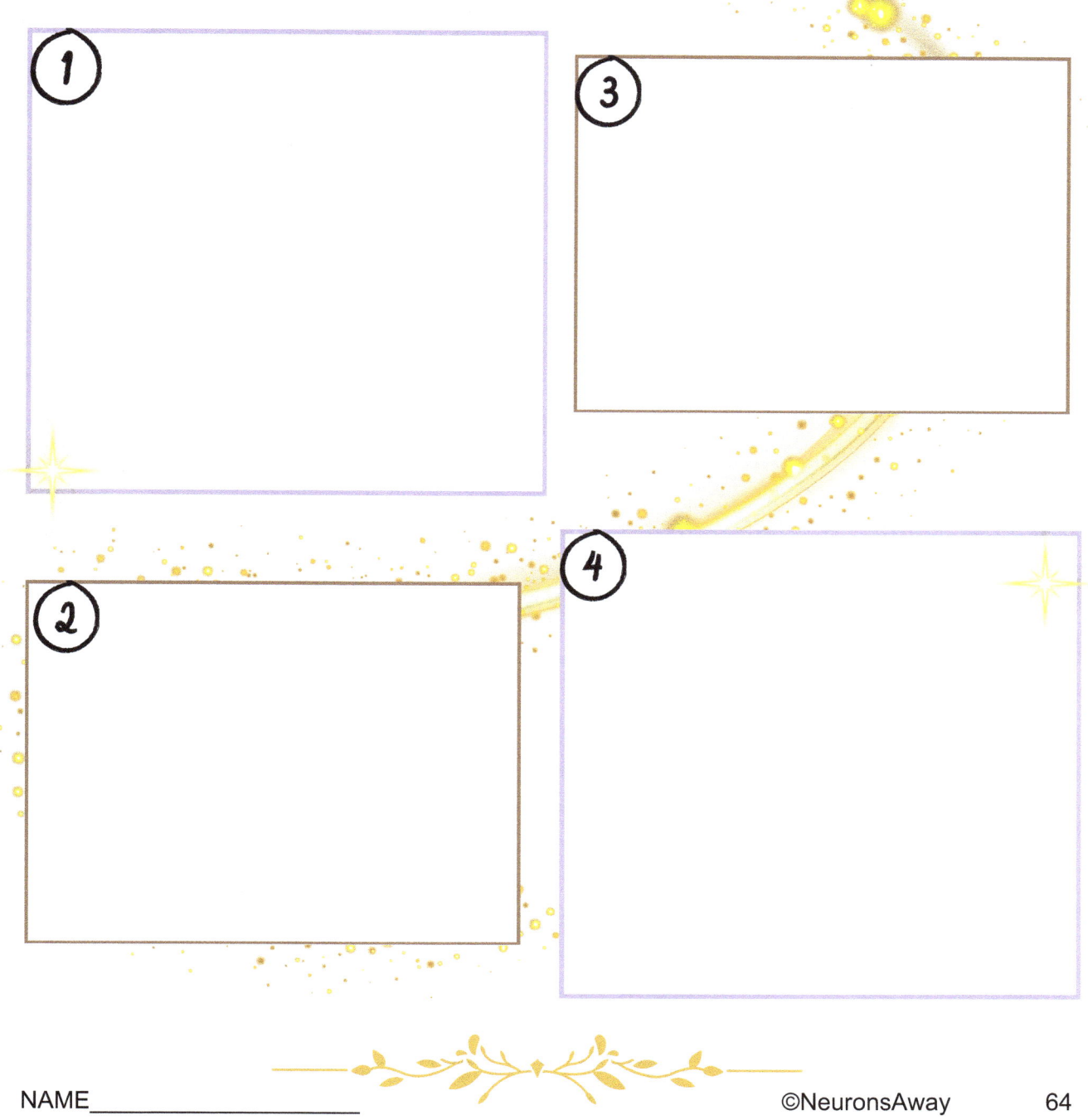

A letter to my younger self. Write a short letter to your younger self.

What advice, encouragement, or wisdom would you share?

SENIOR CARE COGNITIVE ENRICHMENT WORKSHEETS

The Soundtrack of My Life

♫ List three songs that bring back strong memories. Next to each one, write down why it's meaningful to you.

1
_____

2
_____

3
_____

If you could travel to any time—past or future—where would you go and why?

_____
_____
_____
_____
_____
_____

Describe what you would see, do, and experience.

Hope you had fun exercising your mind!

Keep exploring, creating, and reminiscing—your brain will thank you!

KEEP YOUR MIND SHARP!

BUY NOW
Etsy link
TPT link

For Seniors
52 pages

Boost memory and mental agility with activities for seniors in all stages of care.

BUY NOW
Etsy link
TPT link

For Seniors
70 pages

Promote memory care with festive brain games, reflection prompts, and activities.

BUY NOW
Etsy link
TPT link

For Seniors
72 pages

Celebrate fall with memory games, prompts, and puzzles for cognitive health and well-being.

NURTURE YOUR MIND, AT ANY AGE!

BUY NOW
Etsy link
TPT link

For Seniors
70 pages

Engaging activities to boost memory, creativity, and brain health for seniors, including those with dementia.

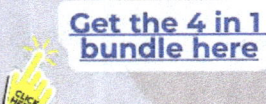

Get the 4 in 1 bundle here

Whether it's memory games or creative challenges, our tools are perfect for enriching your mind and spirit.

neuronsaway.com

Hey there!
Thank you for choosing this workbook to support meaningful activities for seniors. Whether you're a caregiver, family member, therapist, or friend, your dedication makes a world of difference. We create these resources to nurture connection, joy, and growth across all stages of life.

If you found this workbook helpful, we'd love to hear from you! Your feedback and reviews help us improve and continue designing tools that empower seniors and those who care for them. Thank you for your support—it means everything to us!

If you have any feedback please message us at neuronsaway@gmail.com
Thank you

www.ingramcontent.com/pod-product-compliance
Lightning Source LLC
LaVergne TN
LVHW081400060426
835510LV00016B/1912